PROMOTING THE ARTS & SCIENCES:

OPPORTUNITIES TO VOLUNTEER

by Bernard Ryan, Jr.

Ryan, Bernard, 1923-
  Community service for teens: opportunities to volunteer / Bernard
Ryan, Jr.
    p. cm.
  Includes bibliographical references and index.
  Contents: [1] Caring for animals -- [2] Expanding education and
literacy -- [3] Helping the ill, the poor & the elderly -- [4] Increasing
neighborhood service -- [5] Participating in government --
- -[6] Promoting the arts and sciences -- [7] Protecting the environment
- -[8] Serving with police, fire & EMS
    ISBN 0-89434-227-4 (v. 1). -- ISBN 0-89434-231-2 (v. 2). -- ISBN
0-89434-229-0 (v. 3). -- ISBN 0-89434-233-9 (v. 4). --
ISBN 0-89434-230-4 (v. 5). -- ISBN 0-89434-234-7 (v. 6). --
ISBN 0-89434-228-2 (v. 7). -- ISBN 0-89434-232-0 (v. 8)
    1. Voluntarism—United States—Juvenile literature. 2. Young
volunteers—United States—Juvenile literature. 3. Teenage
volunteers in social service—United States—Juvenile literature.
[1. Voluntarism.] I. Title.
HN90.V64R93   1998
361.3'7'08350973—dc21   97-34971
                                                                            CIP
                                                                             AC

Community Service for Teens: Promoting the Arts and Sciences:
Opportunities to Volunteer

A New England Publishing Associates Book
Copyright ©1998 by Ferguson Publishing Company
ISBN 0-89434-234-7

Published and distributed by
Ferguson Publishing Company
200 West Madison, Suite 300
Chicago, Illinois 60606
800-306-9941
Web Site: http://www.fergpubco.com

Printed in the United States of America
V-3

CONTENTS

INTRODUCTION

Six out of ten American teenagers work as volunteers. A 1996 survey revealed that the total number of teen volunteers aged 12 to 17 is 13.3 million. They give 2.4 billion hours each year. Of that time, 1.8 billion hours are spent in "formal" commitments to nonprofit organizations. Informal help, like "just helping neighbors," receives 600 million hours.

Only 16 out of 100 volunteers go to schools that insist on community service before graduation.

Each "formal" volunteer gives an average of three and a half hours a week. It would take nearly 1.1 million full-time employees to match these hours. And if the formal volunteers were paid minimum wage for their time, the cost would come to at least $7.7 billion—a tremendous saving to nonprofit organizations.

Teen volunteerism is growing. In the four years between the 1996 survey and a previous one, the number of volunteers grew by 7 percent and their hours increased by 17 percent.

Equal numbers of girls and boys give their time to volunteering.

How voluntary is volunteering? Only 16 out of 100 volunteers go to schools that insist on community service before graduation. Twenty-six out of 100 are in schools that offer courses requiring community service if you want credit for the course.

Six out of ten teen volunteers started volunteering before they were 14 years old. Seventy-eight percent of teens who volunteer have parents who volunteer.

WHY VOLUNTEER?

When teens are asked to volunteer, the 1996 survey revealed, nine out of ten do so. Who does the asking? Usually a friend, teacher, relative or church member. Teens gave a number of reasons for volunteering, regardless of whether their schools required community service. Their reasons included:

- You feel compassion for people in need.
- You feel you can do something for a cause that is important to you.
- You believe that if you help others, others will help you.
- Your volunteering is important to people you respect.
- You learn to relate to others who may be different from you.
- You develop leadership skills.
- You become more patient.
- You gain a better understanding of good citizenship.
- You get a chance to learn about various careers.
- You gain experience that can help in school and can lead to college admission and college scholarships as well as future careers.

VOLUNTEER FOR WHAT?

You can volunteer in a wide variety of activities. To get a picture of how teen volunteering is spread among various categories, see Exhibit 1 on page 7.

Don't miss an opportunity that is disguised as a requirement.

—Karl Methven, Faculty Member and Head Coach, addressing the Class of 1997, Proctor Academy, Andover, New Hampshire, at the graduation ceremony, May 31, 1997

Exhibit 1

DISTRIBUTION OF TEENS'
VOLUNTEER ACTIVITIES

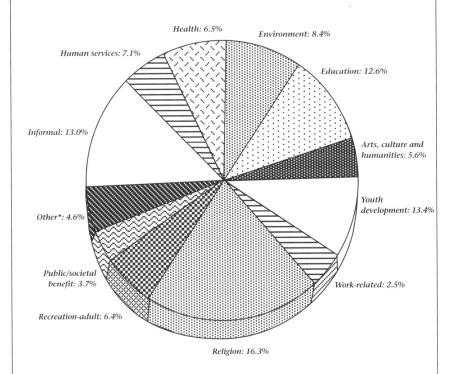

Health: 6.5%

Environment: 8.4%

Human services: 7.1%

Education: 12.6%

Informal: 13.0%

Arts, culture and
humanities: 5.6%

Youth
development: 13.4%

Other*: 4.6%

Public/societal
benefit: 3.7%

Work-related: 2.5%

Recreation-adult: 6.4%

Religion: 16.3%

*Other includes political organizations, international/foreign organizations, private and community foundations and other unspecified
volunteer activity.

(Source: <u>Volunteering and Giving Among American Teenagers: 1996.</u> Independent Sector, Washington,
DC, 1997.)

WHO SAYS YOU HAVE TO "VOLUNTEER"?

Is "volunteering" for community service required in your school? It is if you live in the state of Maryland or in the city of Atlanta, Georgia. In fact, in many school districts across the United States you cannot receive your high school diploma unless you have spent a certain number of hours in community service. The number of hours varies.

Who makes the rule? In Maryland, the only state so far to require every high school student to perform community service, it is the Maryland State Department of Education. In most school districts, it is the board of education, which usually sets policies that meet the standards of the community.

If you have to do it, is it voluntary? And is it legal to make you do it? One family didn't think so. In 1994, the parents of Daniel Immediato, a 17-year-old senior at Rye Neck High School in Mamaroneck, New York, sued in federal court to keep Daniel's school from requiring him to spend 40 hours in community service before he could graduate.

Daniel's parents said the requirement interfered with their right to raise their child, that it violated Daniel's privacy rights, and that it was a violation of the Thirteenth Amendment to the U.S. Constitution. That amendment says:

> Neither slavery nor involuntary servitude, except as a punishment for a crime whereof the party shall have been duly convicted, shall exist within the United States, or any place subject to their jurisdiction.

(Continued on page 9)

(Continued from page 8)

The requirement for community service, said the Immediatos, imposed involuntary servitude on Daniel.

In its defense, the Rye Neck School Board argued that what it wanted was to get the students out into the community to see what goes on in the outside world. In the process, said the board, students would find out what it was like to have to dress appropriately for a job, be on time somewhere and have other people dependent on them. The emphasis was not on what the community would gain, it was on what the student would learn.

The court decided the school system was right. The Immediatos appealed. The U.S. Court of Appeals for the Second Circuit upheld the decision. The Immediatos asked the U.S. Supreme Court to hear the case. It turned down the request, as it does many appeals, without stating its reason for refusing.

"If schools are going to demand that volunteering be part of success as a teenager," says Susan Trafford, president, Habitat for Humanity, Central Westmoreland, Pennsylvania, "I think the teens need to have, first, a selection in the volunteerism that they are going to do, and second, an understanding that this is a responsibility. This is the real world. This isn't the high school. This isn't the halls of Central High. I don't think we can just send them off and say, 'Now, here's your volunteer day.' They need a cause to go there, an understanding of someone, of what they will be contributing to. Sure, there are wonderful things that can be done. But don't send me six who have to do this before they can graduate."

CHAPTER ONE

What Are the Arts and Sciences, and Who Promotes Them?

THE ARTS

*W*hen you think or talk about "the arts" you are getting into a big, broad subject. There is almost no end to what it can include. Yet we must begin somewhere. For the purposes of this book about your opportunities to volunteer, let's begin by thinking about two kinds of people: those who are gifted in the arts and those who support the arts. Not surprisingly, the two are not mutually exclusive: Many people who are talented in the arts are also hard-working supporters of the arts.

Many people who are talented in the arts are also hard-working supporters of the arts.

The arts can range all the way from the fine arts—painting landscapes and portraits and abstract designs, composing music, creating sculpture—to the performing arts, such as you find in dance and theater and orchestra.

You can take each of these arts and put it into either of two main categories. The first is *verbal arts,* the arts that use words. They comprise everything that takes written form. The second is *nonverbal arts.* These are the arts that use design. The design may be for your eyes, your ears or your touch. Design consists of arranging certain elements into a composition. The composition may be two-dimensional, such as a painting, or three-dimensional, such as sculpture. Or it may consist of musical sounds. It may even consist of directing the movement

(Courtesy: Paul Macapia/Seattle Art Museum, Seattle, WA)

Numerous museums and art galleries throughout the United States offer teen volunteers exceptional cultural experiences. Katie Plimpton and another volunteer from the Seattle Art Museum answer questions about antique hair ornaments on display from China.

of performers acting or dancing on the stage.

Some performing arts, of course, combine the verbal and the nonverbal. A play or an opera brings together the words delivered by performers and the visual designs of costumes and settings.

THE SCIENCES

This book explores volunteering in places where people can see and hear some of the elements that make up our culture today and have contributed to its development in the past. It includes not only museums of art but also history museums and museums of natural history. In a sense, the latter come under the umbrella heading of "the sciences" because what they present to the public comes more from the world of the exact sciences than from the world of the creative arts.

If you go to college and set out to earn a bachelor of science degree in any area, you will know that study of the physical sciences deals with hard, objective facts about which there often can be little difference of opinion. If you go for a bachelor of arts degree, on the other hand, you will find that many hours can be spent discussing the humanities and debating what is right or wrong, good or bad, about the myriad aspects of the human condition and how and why we all got where we are today.

The arts and related sciences are all around us in our culture. They invite us to museums, art galleries, concert halls, theaters and historic buildings and sites. They call to us from the past, in the works of great artists over the centuries and the historical development of our culture.

WHY DO THEY NEED HELP?

There are two answers to this question: *money* and *aesthetic experience*. People who are interested help by giving money and working to get others to give money. And they help by working to make the aesthetic experience better and better and to make it available to more and more people. Both kinds of work depend on volunteers to help make them successful.

There is never enough money to pay for the cost of our interest in the arts. Symphonies and other performances sell tickets, often at what seem to be expensive prices. Museums and art galleries open their doors to the public free of charge or at modest admission fees. But in either case, paying the performers and staff people and maintaining the buildings always cost far more than the amounts taken in.

There is never enough money to pay for the cost of our interest in the arts.

The aesthetic experience is what you get out of going to a performance or an exhibition. It is what you see and hear and the intellectual and emotional reaction you have to it.

The goal of people who work in the arts is to make it possible for you and everyone else to keep on having aesthetic experiences. That is why help is needed from you and others.

I think the museum field especially is a great way to learn new facts and meet new people. It's a good thing.
—Coordinator of Volunteers Amanda Rivera Lopez,
Barnum Museum, Bridgeport, Connecticut

WHO CAN HELP?

Help to promote the arts comes from several sources. One is government—national, state and local. Another is philanthropy, which is encouraged by tax breaks offered by the government to individuals and organizations that support the arts and other charitable causes. Yet another source is private organizations that are devoted to the arts. Let's look at some of these.

Much public support for the arts has come through the government. Our elected representatives at national, state and local levels have recognized the importance of the aesthetic experience to our daily lives. They have budgeted dollars that come from taxes to go to the support of the arts through such programs as the National Endowment for the Arts (NEA) and the National Endowment for the Humanities (NEH).

These two independent agencies of the U.S. government were formed in 1965. Since then, each has made grants to artists and nonprofit organizations nationwide and to state and regional arts commissions or agencies. Altogether, the NEA has awarded more than 110,000 fellowships and grants, while the NEH has awarded more than 54,000.

Many states have created commissions on the arts. In Connecticut, for example, the state's Commission on the Arts operated in 1997 on a budget of $3,000,000 and gave $2,321,300 in grants to individuals and organizations.

Cities help, too. Look at San Antonio, Texas, a city of about 1 million people. In 1997, its Department of Arts and Cultural Affairs was spending $2,308,000 of the city's tax receipts to help support the San Antonio Symphony Orchestra and a number of museums. That's $2.31 on behalf of each resident of the city.

NATIONAL, REGIONAL AND LOCAL ORGANIZATIONS

Aside from governments, who else supports the arts? You can find a wide range of private, nonprofit groups that do. Here are a few examples:

- *Friends of the Kennedy Center for the Performing Arts* in Washington pulls in volunteer support for the center and its national outreach programs and other public services.
- The *American Antiquarian Society* gathers and preserves the materials of early American life and its history.

- The *American Institute for Conservation of Historic and Artistic Works* is concerned with the preservation of such cultural property as books, architecture, paintings, photographs, textiles and wooden artifacts.
- The *National Trust for Historic Preservation* is a giant organization that maintains seven regional offices concerned with the preservation of buildings, sites and objects that are meaningful in American history.
- Owning 44 historic sites, with 22 of them operating as museums, the *Society for the Preservation of New England Antiquities* works to preserve and restore architectural landmarks.
- In addition to the national organizations mentioned above, you can find countless state and local *historical societies.* Many operate museums in historic buildings that they own. Often they restore such buildings and make them available for "adaptive use," leasing part or all of the space to bring in rental income. An abandoned railroad station, for example, becomes an art gallery or a real-estate office. A one-room schoolhouse becomes a restaurant.
- Any city or town that provides a symphony orchestra or symphonette to its people is likely to depend on a large organization of supporters. As volunteers, *symphony societies* help with raising funds, selling tickets and planning and running special performance events. Typical projects include "Adult Music Education," "Music for Youth" and "Tiny Tot Music."

WHERE DO YOU SEE OR HEAR THE ARTS?

Buildings seem to add significance and legitimacy to the arts. If you know you are going to see or hear the arts in Carnegie Hall (New York) or the Museum of Modern Art (New York), in the Bushnell Auditorium (Hartford, Connecticut) or the J. Paul Getty

Museum (Los Angeles), in Lincoln Center (New York) or the National Gallery of Art (Washington, D.C.), you know you are in for a treat. But beyond those rather famous names are hundreds and hundreds of buildings across America—concert halls, auditoriums, theaters and art galleries—that are home to the arts. In cities large and small, they make the arts "real" to millions of people every day. Almost all are physical places that welcome—and depend on—volunteers. Not every one offers opportunities for teenagers to volunteer, but many do.

Museums fall into one of three general types: art, history and science museums. The last two reach over from the arts into the humanities, as they are concerned with depicting many aspects of culture.

History Museums

These may be historic houses, such as Mark Twain's home in Connecticut, Thomas Jefferson's in Virginia and Molly Brown's in Denver, Colorado. Or they may be historic villages, such as Virginia's Colonial Williamsburg, Connecticut's Mystic Seaport and Old Sturbridge Village in Massachusetts.

Science Museums

These include museums of natural history (New York's is one of the best known, but you can find many others across the country that are top-notch). Science and technology museums range from the National Air and Space Museum (part of the Smithsonian Institution) in Washington to Chicago's Museum of Science and Industry.

A museum is not a boring place. There is lots of work, very informal kinds of things, to be done.

—Volunteer Coordinator Ben Ortiz,
the Discovery Museum, Bridgeport, Connecticut

16

(V. Harlow)

If you're interested in history, consider volunteering at a living history museum. Connecticut's Mystic Seaport, pictured above, is a popular tourist attraction throughout the year.

CHAPTER TWO

What You'll Do as a Volunteer

*W*hat types of work can you do as a volunteer in the arts? Tasks range from helping within the staff office of a museum or gallery to telling visitors what is significant about a historic building, from raising money in support of a symphony orchestra to selecting items (called *artifacts*) to be included in a museum's latest exhibition.

Many museums or historic sites welcome seventh-graders and up as volunteers.

In the chapters that follow, you will discover a number of community organizations. Many projects and programs will be described, and you will read the thoughts and comments of many individuals, both teens and adults who work with teens. Bear in mind that all the places, projects and people are included as *examples* of what is out there. No two are exactly alike. Most are typical. Some are unusual. But by reading about them you will find out what kinds of opportunities may be waiting just around the corner from you, and you can think about whether similar opportunities would appeal to you.

Many museums or historic sites welcome seventh-graders and up as volunteers. The time you are expected to spend ranges from as little as two or three hours a month during the school year to as much as five half days a week for several weeks in the summer. And in many places you can put in more time if you want to.

When you work as a volunteer in most places, you really become a member of the staff. That means you are valuable to the community organization you volunteer for—museum, gallery, orchestra, theater or historic site. You play an important role.

You may also contribute to a gradual change in philosophy that many such organizations are undergoing. Take it from Ben Ortiz, volunteer coordinator at the Discovery Museum, an art and science museum in Bridgeport, Connecticut. "For many, many years," says Ortiz, "this museum was looked at as part of an ivory-tower kind of thing. That is changing and our philosophy is that this should be part of the younger community." Ortiz explains that the museum has been working with inner-city children through several programs, including one that taught them about historical preservation. This summer's project was so successful that it lasted into the autumn. When the project was over, Ortiz found the teens had a different outlook and increased respect for historic preservation and for American history.

"We're connecting with the youth, especially in the city," reports Ortiz, "so they see that this is their museum and they should share in the work as part of their community." Ortiz finds that the volunteer work gives teens a sense of community, of pride and spirit. He sees them as "the caretakers of the next generation."

Ortiz says that more than half of all volunteers at the Discovery Museum are teenagers. "They're really great," he says. "Some are Hispanic, and I talk with them in Spanish and show them that Hispanics, or any minority, can be part of this."

Now let's look at some of the areas in which you can be a valuable volunteer.

FUND-RAISING

Any community organization has to raise money on a regular basis. This is tough work. Some adults never get used to it. Even after years of working for nonprofit organizations that run annual drives, some find themselves tongue-tied or just plain embarrassed when asking for money.

An organization you volunteer with may or may not include teenagers in its fund-raising. If yours does, that does not mean you will be forced to do this kind of work. But you may be offered the chance to learn how to do it in training sessions. If that happens, it will give you a good chance to find out what kind of salesperson you are and whether you have an interest in selling in the future. Selling, especially the selling of an intangible such as the aesthetic experience, is a special talent. It can be learned and developed, but it is not for everyone.

LEARNING HOW A MUSEUM OPERATES

"I explain to the kids exactly how their jobs fit into the museum's scheme of things," says Amanda Rivera Lopez, coordinator of volunteers at the Barnum Museum in Bridgeport, Connecticut. Lopez finds that teens who perform office work get a good understanding of how the museum operates.

"If you are stuffing envelopes with membership applications," Lopez says, "you quickly understand that that supports the financial base of the museum.

"Any kind of experience," she adds, "really helps you decide what ultimately you want to do in the future and the kind of work you are good at."

At the Barnum Museum, a junior volunteer program officially accepts teens who are 14 and up. Most of what they do is behind the scenes, such as helping to prepare materials for various family programs. Teens help out in the office. The most adventurous participate as what are called gallery attendants, people available in the gallery to answer questions about the exhibits, to help families use the interactive exhibits and to answer questions and give directions.

Some teens at Barnum are called education assistants. They are in charge of leading and teaching crafts activities, mostly on school vacation days.

SPECIAL EVENTS

Many museums and performance groups put on special events to help attract large numbers of people. These may be held in the evening or on a Saturday, Sunday or holiday—times when school is not in session, so that whole families can attend. The events can range from parties for those who support the organization financially to lectures and demonstrations on art or history related to a specific exhibition. Teen volunteers help with preparing and serving refreshments, leading tours, parking cars, taking tickets, setting up seating arrangements and cleaning up afterward.

HELP RECRUIT VOLUNTEERS

Another activity in which you can help is in the recruitment of volunteers like you. Many schools put on *volunteer fairs* once or twice a year. They invite local or area organizations that need volunteers to come in and set up booths or displays that explain who does what and why they do it in their particular kind of community service. If you are already a dedicated volunteer, you can help get your peers or younger students interested. "I work with a lot of local community organizations that participate in volunteer fairs," says Amanda Lopez, of the Barnum Museum. When Lopez goes to a fair, she takes any kids who are from the school that is having the fair and who are already volunteers at her museum. They sit with her in the booth and help with recruitment. "Their peers see them doing their thing, like putting up a poster in the guidance department, talking the place up in their school. That works pretty well," notes Lopez.

WHAT IT TAKES TO VOLUNTEER

What it takes to work in these areas is, first, good physical condition. You should have a high level of energy. Your assignment in a gallery or museum may demand that you spend three or four hours on a Saturday or Sunday on your feet with your brain fully in gear as you comment on the exhibits people have come to see and to ask questions about.

You should have a high level of energy.

How old do you have to be? That depends. Junior volunteers at a "living-history" site such as Colonial Williamsburg or Old Sturbridge Village may start as young as nine. But for most of the volunteer opportunities you must be at least a ninth-grader—age 14 or so.

COMMITMENT COUNTS

As in any volunteer activity, you can be sure the professionals you work with will expect dependability more than anything else. They don't want to spend their time training you if they cannot rely on you to be there when you say you'll be there and do what you say you'll do.

What makes you dependable is your own interest in the work. Do you have a strong interest in art, music, history or science? Are you thinking of becoming a teacher? An anthropologist? Does the whole field of education and learning appeal to you? Your interest in one or more of these subjects will dictate your commitment to helping others enjoy the aesthetic experience.

But your commitment does not mean giving up *all* your free time. No well-run volunteer program expects that. "I discourage

(Courtesy: Colonial Williamsburg Foundation, Williamsburg, VA)

Colonial Williamsburg is a popular place to visit, especially in the summer season. During the slower part of the year, volunteers may do maintenance work. This boy is painting the shutters at the Geddy House.

five days a week," says Maria Bagg, coordinator of volunteers at Mystic Seaport in Connecticut. "We're not a baby-sitting service, and we don't want to have parents dropping their kids off early and picking them up late in the afternoon." Bagg notes that this is unfair to the museum staff. While Mystic Seaport is a fun place to be, you should also be having, as Bagg puts it, "some goof-off days." She asks for a commitment of at least one day a week, and finds that many of her teen volunteers come to work for three or four. Since Mystic Seaport is open seven days a week, many of them are there on the weekends.

"We expect you here at least one day per week in the summer and holidays, and during spring break and Christmas vacation," says Judy Kupfer, manager of volunteer programs at the Chicago Museum of Science and Industry. During the school year, teen volunteers put in either a Saturday or a Sunday twice a month. "We do depend on you to be here," she tells them. "It is a part of the program. You are scheduled in. It's a commitment on your part and on our part."

WHAT SKILLS MUST YOU BRING? WHAT TRAINING WILL YOU GET?

The most valuable skills you can bring to volunteering in the arts are "people skills"—the ability to get along with others, understand their points of view and put across your point of view on any issue.

The ability to get on your feet and speak to a group is also important. Not every volunteer has to be a good public speaker, but if you have this skill—or can master it—you will have an advantage. If, for example, you want to work as an interpreter or docent explaining an exhibit or a historic building to visitors, you will be at a real disadvantage if you are uncomfortable speaking to groups.

Other useful skills? Every organization needs help in the day-to-day work in the office—typing, filing, entering data in the computer. If you are comfortable handling telephone calls—can speak clearly, explain carefully and listen alertly—you offer a skill that not everyone brings to the office.

How do the coordinators of teen volunteers describe the qualifications they look for? Judy Kupfer puts it very simply: "We treat our volunteers as if they were employees." If you apply for volunteer work at the Chicago Museum of Science and Industry, you will be interviewed first by someone from the volunteer office. Then you will meet with someone in the department you want to work in. If that's a "fit," you go to work. If not, they try to find another place for you.

Every organization needs help in the day-to-day work in the office.

Amanda Lopez, of the Barnum Museum, says, "It depends on what kind of thing you're interested in doing." She conducts a formal interview process, checking to match the teenager's interests against the museum's needs. "My philosophy is that it's got to be mutual. If I have a student who is interested in doing work out front but I don't feel he or she has any people skills, I will try and have that person do something behind the scenes until he or she develops those skills," says Lopez.

The qualification requirements may be quite simple. Cathy Andreychek, coordinator of teens at the Carnegie Museum of Natural History in Pittsburgh, sends out application packages to most of the schools in the Pittsburgh vicinity, concentrating on middle schools. The kids have to be at least 13 years old. They need recommendations from teachers and they must see Andreychek for an interview and fill out an application.

HOW MUCH TRAINING?

How much training you are likely to get—or to need—depends on the place where you are volunteering. A large museum or gallery may include several extensive floors of exhibition space. Particular shows or exhibits may bring with them complex background information that you must learn about so that, as a docent or interpreter, you can do your job well.

If kids just want to do office work but I see there is great potential to do other things, I will strongly encourage them to take on a new challenge. Sometimes kids have a lot of talent but they are just a little shy about using it and just need a little help.

—Coordinator of Volunteers Amanda Lopez,
Barnum Museum,
Bridgeport, Connecticut

YOUR ATTITUDE AND INTEREST

Any coordinator of volunteers is going to expect you to have a positive attitude toward the work. That means you cannot be shy about tackling any particular assignment or about dealing with people, whether they are employees behind the scenes or members of the public coming to see the exhibits or sit in the audience for a performance.

DON'T OVERDO IT

The adults who coordinate the work of teen volunteers don't want you to spread yourself too thin. "We find that it's a good compromise if the kids do three hours a week in the summertime and three hours a month during the school year," says Peggy Beidelman, volunteer coordinator at the Chicago Children's Museum. She says that otherwise demands may become too high and you may not be able to keep your commitment. "We don't want you to end up feeling disappointed or like you've let us down," Beidelman says, "so we try to keep it to a realistic level."

CHAPTER THREE

Volunteering in History, Natural History and Science Museums

A re you interested in how people lived during the American Revolution or the Civil War or at other times in the past? Or does natural history, the study of living creatures in nature, interest you? Many museums are devoted to local or regional history and many specialize in the science of natural history.

"AN UNUSUAL FOCUS"

At the Naval Undersea Museum in Keyport, Washington, teens aged 13 to 16 do many jobs. Primarily the program began by using teens to handle the crowds that came in during the busy summer months. The museum management quickly found that the teenagers had enthusiasm and skills in all areas of the museum. They work in education, reading stories to young children and working with younger children who tour the museum in groups. In the summer of 1997, they made a fun job of creating a mural in the education section. They work in the curator's office, registering artifacts and doing data input in the computer. In the library, they shelve books and make copies and handle other clerical tasks.

"One of the things I was very surprised to find when we started the program," says educator and Volunteer Programs Manager Joyce

(Naval Undersea Museum, Keyport, Washington)

Tyler Kaye performs many tasks as a volunteer at the Naval Undersea Museum in Keyport, Washington. Tyler (right) and a friend work on a yellow submarine cutout for an upcoming children's program.

Jensen, "was the response. Many schools require some sort of community service. The students were eager because we have an unusual focus—the biology and the technology of the underseas. It's just a little different from the usual volunteer job in the hospital or wherever."

Jensen found the teen volunteers eager to learn new skills. In the program's first three years, it lost very few volunteers. The teens all stayed throughout the summers, with 30 of them contributing 1,700 hours to the museum.

Ninth-grader Tyler Kaye volunteered at the Naval Undersea Museum in the summer of 1997. He worked at the museum two days a week, each Friday and Saturday, from late June to the end of August. Much of his time was spent in the curator's office. "The museum is trying to become an accredited museum," he says. "In order to do that it has to have all its items cataloged." Tyler explains, "One of my most important tasks was database entry. I would enter the items and other staff members would make copies for the tax records of people who donated things."

Tyler also worked as a gallery attendant. With the museum showing an art collection on loan from Washington, D.C., his duties included keeping an eye on the paintings and greeting visitors to the floor. He also worked in the facility's storage area, keeping things in order and cleaning up.

Tyler's favorite part of the work was in the curator's office. "I just enjoyed the data entry and seeing the variety of artifacts that are at the museum that the average person doesn't get to see". Among his favorite artifacts are the museum's large collection of diving helmets and other diving paraphernalia that go back to 1893, as well as various items from early submarines.

Teen volunteers have to fill out the same application that adult volunteers fill out. The form looks like a job application and requires references, phone numbers, prior work experience if you have any, and prior volunteer experience. We also conduct a face-to-face interview.

—**Educator and Volunteer Programs Manager Joyce Jensen, Naval Undersea Museum, Keyport, Washington**

"DOING DISSECTIONS AND ASSISTING TEACHERS IN THE CLASSROOM"

To give you an idea of what you might be doing as a teen volunteer in a fairly large-scale operation, let's look in on the Denver, Colorado, Museum of Natural History. There you will find from 1,800 to 2,000 volunteers of all ages. Some are younger than the museum's minimum of 14, so they come in with their parents or grandparents to volunteer.

A special teen program takes youths aged 14 to 18. While its primary focus in the past has been on summertime work, says Teen Volunteer Coordinator Vicki Leigh, it is developing more and more as a year-round opportunity. In the summer of 1997, the Denver program included about 80 teens working in 24 different departments of the museum.

Leigh says the largest group of teens worked as teacher's assistants in the museum's Youth Program, helping in a variety of natural history classes. Another large group were teacher's assistants in the *Hall of Life,* an exhibition on biology and the body. "They helped with all sorts of different things," says Leigh, "even doing dissections and assisting teachers in the classroom."

A third, large group of teens worked in Gallery Presentations. There they handled touch carts—small wagons loaded with artifacts that visitors may examine while the teens in charge explain them.

Other teens worked as research assistants. "They were helping a paleontologist," Leigh reports, "and working with people in zoology." These volunteers were given the opportunity to participate in fieldwork. They also worked as office assistants and helped out in photo labs. "So it's kind of all over," says Leigh, "depending on what needs the staff has for the year."

When asked, "What does the museum get out of the teen volun-

The Denver program included about 80 teens working in 24 different departments.

(Courtesy: Rick Wicker/Denver Museum of Natural History, Denver, CO)

At the Denver, Colorado, Museum of Natural History, teachers present various workshops in the Hall of Life, an exhibition on biology and the body. Assisting the teachers are two volunteers who prepare to thaw out animal organs to be used in a workshop on biology.

teer effort?" Leigh recounts the evolution of her program. When it first started as a summer project in 1991, the museum staff was hesitant about it. "We didn't want to just have bodies here," she says. "We wanted to make sure they had an educational experience."

While it took some time to put the program together, the staff people soon realized how much energy the teens had and how hard they worked. They discovered that the teens, as Leigh puts it, "brought creativity into the institution and the program just took on a life of its own. People started getting excited and the staff really built on that."

Now the Denver museum's teen program has become year-round. Leigh finds one staff member after another coming in to ask for the help of teen volunteers. "And that," she says, "really makes it fun."

Now that the teen program has become fully accepted, Leigh finds that evaluations she gets from the staff show that they are delighted about working with the teens. In the school year 1996–97, she estimates, requests from the museum staff for teen volunteers increased by about 60 percent.

Leigh mentions something that seemed to be an obstacle to the teen volunteer program at first. Some of the museum's adult volunteers, many of whom are retired, felt uneasy about the teen program. To work on the relationships between the generations, some of the older volunteers were appointed as mentors to the teens. And in May of each year, a "How to Work with a Teen" workshop is held. All staff supervisors of teens, as well as some adult volunteers, are invited. The workshop concentrates on how to work with teens, what teens are going through physically, what kinds of behavior they engage in and what is the best way to supervise them. "That gives our adults a chance to voice any concerns that they might have," says Leigh.

FIELD TRIPS AND ICE CORES

At the Denver museum or any other, when you first start, you must get familiar with the particular place. "After the interview process," says Leigh, "there's an overall orientation with the whole group. You learn about the museum and our rules and regulations and you get a tour of the facility." Since you can expect to work a lot of the time directly with museum visitors, you learn about customer service. And you get to know the other teenage volunteers.

Next, volunteers in training get individual orientations with each of the departments. If you are going to be a teacher's assistant, for example, you will learn all about the classrooms and the different classes you will be teaching and meet the teachers themselves.

In addition to that training, at the Denver museum teen volunteers go on a field trip every Friday throughout the summer. They visit all the nearby science and cultural-related organizations, like the art museum, or Dinosaur Ridge, where many fossils have been found. Or they might go hiking and learn about the flora and fauna in some outdoor area. One popular trip is to the National Ice Core Lab—the ice and geologic resource lab. Scientists there drill downward to look at hundreds of thousands of years of weather patterns recorded in the ice.

"It's very interesting for teens to learn this way," says Leigh, "because we're trying to show them that a museum involves a lot of different disciplines. You have the frontline people but you also have the paleontologists and the photographers and the marketing people—all these people in different types of careers work together."

Another frequent and popular event that occurs several times during a summer of volunteering at the Denver museum is lunchtime with staff people. At each lunch, the teen volunteers get an opportunity to meet with four or five people who represent various departments within the museum.

We look at our teens as people who are thinking about science or culture as a career, so we emphasize careers in this program. We want to make sure that they are really interested and want to be here.

—**Teen Volunteer Coordinator Vicki Leigh,**
Denver Museum of Natural History

THREE TIERS OF VOLUNTEERS

Now let's stop in at the Fort Worth Museum of Science and History in Texas, where Karen Turner is director of special programs. The museum works regularly with about 40 to 50 teenagers aged 13 to 17. Turner explains that while teens gain valuable lessons from their volunteering experience, the museum reaps two important benefits.

First, the museum gets the satisfaction of introducing young teens to the work effort that is needed to support the aesthetic experience. "Our group is not a large one," says Turner, "but the goal of the program is to provide the youngsters with a first-time work experience, help them build job skills, gain some knowledge in science and history and learn to work in a different environment from what they're used to in their school or their home life."

Turner describes the museum's teen program as "three tiered." At the first level, she says, teens may volunteer for at least a year in a number of different capacities, most of which involve working with the public. This is a sort of training period, working both with teen peers and with adult volunteers.

After they have worked at the museum for at least a year, teen volunteers can apply for an internship. This is a summer opportunity, where they work for two and a half to three months in a particular

department at the museum. The job can be in the museum's education department, in its museum school, in exhibits or in the collections area. "This tier gives them a little more responsibility," says
Turner. "It's more of a real working environment, and they get paid
a small stipend for putting in so many hours a month."

At the third tier, after the teens are 16 and have worked with the
museum for several years, they can apply for part-time positions.
While they get first consideration, however, they are not guaran-
teed a job or an internship. "The kids who stick with it," Turner
explains, "are generally kids that we would like to hire, so they
become a very good pool of candidates for some of our part-time
positions." In effect, this is another benefit the museum gets from
the teen volunteer program: a readily available supply of well-
trained, interested and knowledgeable workers.

"DINO DIGS" AND FAMILY SCIENCE NIGHTS

What kinds of jobs might you be doing in a museum like the one in
Forth Worth? You could be working on various special projects. For
example, you could develop exhibits for a series of small display
cases in the education wing, where younger visitors come through,
often in groups from schools. You could go out on field-trip digs to
stock fossils for the "Dino Dig," an in-house exhibit where kids can
dig in the sand and find fossils. On special-event days, you may be
doing everything from greeting the public and handing out information to working at the special tables where you present some
simple kinds of science demonstrations.

A typical special event is "Family Science Night" with the Fort
Worth school district. This is an opportunity for a school to bring all
its children and their parents to the museum for an evening of fun.
The event gets them acquainted with the museum and with infor-

(Courtesy: Fort Worth Museum of Science and History, Fort Worth, TX)

At the Fort Worth Museum of Science and History in Texas, volunteers enjoy a number of different activities while working with the public. This group of teenagers helps to bury "fresh bones" in the museum's popular "Dino Dig" exhibit.

mal learning in science. The teens help with everything from parking to demonstrations to serving refreshments.

Turner says some special programming goes on in conjunction with the exhibits, and the teens help with that. For example, for an exhibit on the animal supersenses, teen volunteers worked in a number of different hands-on activities and spoke to visiting family groups about the eyes of the owl, the ears of the whale or the sensitive nose of the dog.

You will find that a museum like this runs a wide gamut of exhibitions—from hands-on science to history exhibits. The exhibits change three times a year, so the subject matter you learn about and work with depends on the current exhibits. A recent exhibit at the Fort Worth museum, "A Flagship Speaks—the Wreck of the *Henrietta Marie*," featured historical artifacts from the early slave trade in the Americas. The *Henrietta Marie* was a slave ship that sank off the coast of Florida in 1700. The artifacts recovered from the wreck site, says Turner, speak eloquently to the middle passage—the slave trade from western Africa to the Americas. The museum set up guided tours of the exhibit for the general public as well as school groups, with several activity stations in the exhibit where people could make African masks. The museum's teen volunteers worked in all such hands-on areas, helping to get the visitors who came through the exhibit directly involved in it.

How enthusiastic are you about the aesthetic experience an organization like the Fort Worth Museum of Science and History is offering to the public? As Turner says, "Our teen coordinator does the interviews and she will determine if she thinks a teen is really interested in the program. Sometimes we get teens who are just joining because their friends are here. We can't have an unlimited number at one time, so we have to be selective."

LOGGING PAPERWORK, DESIGNING EXHIBITS, MOVING TEXTILES

At 15, Laurel Simmons is in her third year as a volunteer at the Fort Worth Museum of Science and History. Home-schooled, she finds time to spend four hours a week at the museum (during the summer months, she gives eight hours a week).

Laurel explains that she does everything from logging paperwork to helping design some exhibits. For example, she worked for some weeks in the history department, helping to prepare the exhibit on the slave ship *Henrietta Marie*. And before that she helped get a Hispanic heritage exhibit ready to be mounted in an off-site building. Another project Laurel enjoyed was working with various textiles and designing displays to be installed in glass cases. "The fun," she says, "was in getting the artifacts we wanted to use and putting them in the design that we thought would look best."

That's not all. For a long time, says Laurel, the volunteers were working on moving textiles from one form of storage to another. Some were antique textiles; others, more modern quilts and flags. "That took up probably about the first year or so that I was in the department," she says. "We had so many and we had to roll them versus just hanging them. The project took quite a long time."

TEETH, CLAWS AND FOOTPRINTS

At the Carnegie Museum of Natural History in Pittsburgh, Cathy Andreychek, coordinator of the teen docent program, has teens 13 through 17 working as interpreters. They interact with the visiting public, discuss exhibits, tell visitors about the animals they are seeing in the exhibits and use a variety of hands-on items to help with the whole process of interaction.

For example, in the museum's Dinosaur Hall, teen volunteers can show visitors a number of fossil replicas, dinosaur teeth, claws and footprints. In the Hall of African Wildlife, they show—and explain—animal skulls, skins, insects and musical instruments from Africa. They conduct what are called "minitours," where they work from carts that carry touchable items they can talk about. "As they become more comfortable with their surroundings and what they're doing," says Andreychek, "they venture from behind the cart and begin to do brief 10- or 15-minute talks in the hall, maybe at a particular diorama or at a particular dinosaur."

If your enthusiasm wanes, you are going to start to lose interest.

What does the museum coordinator look for in teen volunteers? Andreychek wants to see an enthusiastic interest in the place, the exhibits, the interpreting, and the visitors or audience. "If they are going to stay in this program," she says, "they have to maintain a level of enthusiasm." Her experience is that if your enthusiasm wanes, you are going to start to lose interest. So every month she sends the teen volunteers a questionnaire asking about days in the next month when they can be available. If she does not hear from a particular teen for three months, she sends a letter asking if the teen wants to continue in the program.

At the Carnegie Museum, high school senior Lindsey Shaginaw volunteers as a teen docent. She works in various exhibition areas—the Hall of African Wildlife, for example, or the Hall of Dinosaurs. She has had several weeks of training on the exhibitions in each of

(Courtesy: Carnegie Museum of Natural History, Pittsburgh, PA)

A teen docent at the Carnegie Museum of Natural History in Pittsburgh, Pennsylvania, shows some children fossil replicas from the Hall of African Wildlife.

the halls and on their particular touchables carts. "When the kids come in," she says, "I'm in the hall with the cart and I show them everything that's in it. And I tell people about the exhibitions in the hall."

Lindsey has other duties that add variety to her work and to the patrons' visits. She runs games for the younger children, even dressing, on occasion, in a gorilla costume to supervise a scavenger hunt throughout the museum.

Suppose you volunteer at the Carnegie Museum. How intensive will your training be? Andreychek requires you to be there for six Saturdays of training, starting in the Hall of African Wildlife. The sessions run from 9:30 to 2:00. This is when you learn not only about the hall, but also about interacting. In fact, you do many activities that help you get ready for talking with people. After the six Saturdays, you are given some tests as well as homework. Then you start a regular schedule as a teen docent.

A few months later, you get more training, which requires three days. This time it is in Dinosaur Hall. Usually it is done during the summer, so you can train on weekdays. Is it intensive? "It has to be that way," says Andreychek, "and I'm just amazed at the enthusiasm, and that they all do it. After they've been through six Saturdays during the school year, they can't wait for their dinosaur training."

It takes interesting work to keep any volunteer showing up regularly. Most coordinators of volunteers are aware of that. They know you may become discouraged very quickly if the routine is always the same. "Keeping the subject material fresh is a problem," says Andreychek. "We continue to add new things to their carts so they're not saying the same things over and over, because that gets boring for them." And the museum installs new exhibits every summer, giving teen volunteers the opportunity to add something new to their base of knowledge.

THE CHICAGO MUSEUM OF SCIENCE AND INDUSTRY

Judy Kupfer, manager of volunteer programs at the Chicago Museum of Science and Industry, says, "If you're 15 or older, you can work in our exhibits as an 'exhibit explainer.' We use a lot of volunteers in what we call our 'temp zone.' That's for 'temporary.' It handles visiting exhibits that keep on changing."

The Chicago museum offers patrons a wide range of exhibits. Teen volunteers have explained everything from an extensive review of automobiles and their history to "Christmas Around the World", which is an annual event. They have delighted in the challenge of a Lego exhibit. They explained a two-year-long, temporary exhibit, *Fantastic Machines,* which was made up of objects that people might have used a hundred years ago. When the movie *Jurassic Park* was popular, the museum mounted a *Jurassic Park* exhibit. It gave the teens the opportunity to describe to visitors what life was like for a prehistoric animal.

For every new exhibit that comes into the temp zone, the teens have one or two days of training. They learn the science of whatever the subject is, and what the museum expects them to know—answers to the typical questions they can expect to be asked. "And in addition," says Kupfer, "when they're just interfacing with the visitors, they can do the 'pocket demonstration.' Usually this demonstration is used while people are waiting in line, if there are lines. The teens show the people the maze of mazes. It's a puzzle of metal links that are hooked together."

A HANDS-ON VIEW OF HISTORY

"I volunteer in the Discovery Place," says high-school senior Ellen Thompson, who gives her time to the Kansas Museum of History in Topeka. "The museum has a bunch of displays for kids to play with and get a hands-on view of Kansas history. We help them under-stand the history of telephone development, for example, by using old telephones that still work."

Among other exhibits where teen docents greet visitors and con-duct tours is a place where they can sit and listen to various musi-cal instruments. A display of midwestern geography lights up and shows where Native Americans originally came from and how they moved across Kansas. Another exhibit invites visitors to try on clothes from different periods and dress up.

We look for teens who will take the job seriously. When we recruit, we tell school counselors that we're not looking for the gifted, we're not looking for the most talented, we're just looking for students who would like an experience in a museum.
—Director of Education Mary Madden,
Kansas Museum of History, Topeka

The museum runs a six-week program for volunteers aged 13 to 15, from the last week in June to the first week in August. Mary Madden, who supervises the teens, says the museum recruits up to 30 students to interpret the exhibits in the 20,000-square-foot main gallery, which presents the history of Kansas from the prehistoric period to the present. The gallery includes a full complement of Native American objects and a Santa Fe train.

The tours, led by teen explainers, take visitors through various topics in Kansas history, such as railroads, or cowboys or the Ore-gon Trail experience. During the one-hour tours, the teens use many hands-on objects. "For example," says Madden, "our Civil War tour has a sergeant's uniform and a haversack." As in other museums, if you are a teen explainer here, you work with touch carts and become well trained in the skills of getting visitors

(Courtesy: Chicago Museum of Science and Industry)

A teen volunteer at the Chicago Museum of Science and Industry demonstrates the principles of weight and balance to a young man visiting "The Idea Factory," an exhibit for children.

involved. You encourage them to play an old-fashioned, cup-and-ball game or pick up the flatiron and feel its heft a few times. You give them a different learning experience that helps them understand how hard women worked in the 19th century.

The teens go through four hours of training a day for three days. It's very intensive. That's when they get their crash course on Kansas history, how to handle the public and how to be a good interpreter.
                    —**Director of Education Mary Madden,**
                            Kansas Museum of History, Topeka

MINI-HISTORIANS

Some museums offer very active programs for visiting groups from schools. At the Dakota Prairie Museum in Aberdeen, South Dakota, junior docents—who are mostly 12 and 13 years old—study local landmarks or old-fashioned toys or dolls and other artifacts. Sherri Rawstern, coordinator of teen volunteers, says, "They rehearse and rehearse, and then they get up four at a time in front of a visiting group and talk about some portion of history." Rawstern says the young teens "really become mini-historians." And she finds that they come back year after year. In the summer of 1997, for example, she had two 15-year-olds helping her with several programs. "They remember it," she says. "They retain it, they really have a love of it."

CHAPTER FOUR
Volunteering in Living-History Sites

SUMMER OUTDOOR WORK

Does your volunteering have to be in a big city museum with giant halls? No. Smaller historic sites, for example, are almost everywhere and most of them welcome volunteer help. High-school senior Kate Sands has volunteered at the Stanley-Whitman House in Farmington, Connecticut, since fifth grade. "It's a small historical museum," she says. "I'm in the Junior Docent program, giving the talk and taking people around the three rooms on the first floor and the two rooms upstairs." During the summer, Kate helps with a program called "Dooryard Days," in which she and other volunteers depict various historic scenes each day. One day it will be open-hearth cooking, and another day they stage a birthday party. Or they take visitors out into the dooryard (an area just outside the door of a house) and talk about the herbs in the garden.

A TRIP TO MYSTIC

Such "living-history" sites—large and small—are becoming more common throughout the United States. One of the oldest and largest is Mystic Seaport, a nationally known museum and historic site in Connecticut. Let Maria Bag, manager, volunteer services and staff development, be your guide on a tour of the opportunities for teens at Mystic:

"Let's start in the planetarium. We have junior volunteers who help our planetarium director by preparing and presenting talks on the stars and the planets. And in the planetarium office, they do some filing and clerical tasks.

"At our summer camp we have a group that helps with the arts and crafts. They take on special projects when a rainy day drives everyone indoors. Generally this attracts young people who want to be teachers one day.

"Now, here in the Children's Museum, for children seven and under, several young volunteers help the teachers. They do everything from stamp on what we like to call "tattoos," to teaching how to tie knots, to explaining the aquarium. They also help teach kids how to walk on stilts and how to play with hoops and some of the other games from the 1800s.

"They take the summer campers down to our Australia Beach, where they help the younger children see what they can catch in their nets and traps. They talk about the little critters the kids might find, and show them such things as the difference between one kind of jelly fish and another.

"Now, at the seaport, we have young people who work as helpers on the ships. They're not really deckhands. They help the demonstration squad—a group of paid staff members who raise and lower the lifeboats and go aloft and set the sails. And the junior volunteer who's helping them is coiling ropes and doing some crowd control and maybe loosening the jib. We don't let the teen volunteers go aloft, of course. But they help on deck.

"During the winter holidays, when we do evening, lantern-light tours, we often have young volunteers take roles in the story we tell. Say you're a visitor. You are met at the gate by a staff person in costume with a lantern.

You ride in a horse-drawn buggy to the first stop. It's a progressive story, usually with a Christmas theme to it, and Santa Claus always appears at one point along the way. Visitors end up in the tavern having cocoa and cookies and dancing to the fiddlers. The teen volunteers enjoy getting all dressed up for our visitors and re-creating Mystic Seaport as it once was.

"Now here we are at the boat livery, where we rent out small boats. We have a group of teenagers who help with the life jackets and do everything here. This morning I came down to check on a young fellow and there he was pumping the rainwater out of the boats and wiping them down. And the teens help with the classes and show people how to row. It's a fun duty. They get to sail a lot themselves if they know how to sail.

"Many of our teens have more than one duty. They might work two days a week in the planetarium and two days in the boat livery, or one day with the demonstration squad and another day with the Children's Museum. I try to give them a bit of variety in what they're doing. It rounds them out so they get to have all kinds of experiences."

MEETING INTERESTING PEOPLE

Maybe you are lucky enough to live near a unique museum or historic site that not only draws visitors from far and wide but also has remarkable staff members and adult volunteers. That can mean "fantastic benefits" for you, according to Bag. "Our teen volunteers not only get experience they would never get in other places," she says. "Working here with our paid staff and our regular volunteer staff, they are exposed to the most wonderful people with the

(Courtesy: Mystic Seaport, Mystic, CT)

Teen volunteers participate in the lantern-light tour, part of the holiday celebration at Mystic Seaport.

most diverse and highly accomplished backgrounds." At Mystic Seaport, she says, you can be working with the former CEO of a major corporation, or with a retired admiral, or with someone who landed fighter jets on the carrier deck in World War II or maybe with a woman who circumnavigated the globe with her family.

A GREAT FEELING

What do teen volunteers have to say about why they give their precious time? Let's find out from Eddie Murphy, a high school sophomore who volunteers at Mystic Seaport.

Over two summers and the winter between, Eddie has worked in several areas of Mystic Seaport. The summer of 1997 found him

49

there six days a week. Doing what? "A variety of things," says Eddie. He worked in interpretation, explaining the seaport and its history to visitors. He taught rowing and sailing. And at the planetarium, he helped track the seaport's weather.

Eddie sees two important reasons for volunteering. "First," he says, "it probably will help me to get a job at the seaport in the future. And second, it allows me to help the people who come to the seaport to understand about the boats here and the great heritage that we have in maritime history. It's an incredible place of learning. It has enormous facilities for research and the development of information on how the traditional ships and boats evolved into more modern forms."

Does Eddie anticipate a future in the maritime world? Probably. He expects to go to college in a couple of years, then return to the seaport. And he adds that he "most certainly" thinks his Mystic Seaport work will be helpful on applications to college.

How about specific skills that he has learned right there? Eddie says there are two he considers "major ones." First, his experience helped him understand the rules of seamanship. But even more important, he says, he developed "the skill of dealing with the visitors and teaching them about watercraft and the many aspects of seamanship and maritime life."

Eddie says the best tip he can give to somebody thinking about any kind of volunteering is this: "It's a great experience to help any organization. To give time and also give of whatever resources you have—from your previous knowledge or prior experience. It's a great feeling to be helping others with your time."

A VISIT TO COLONIAL WILLIAMSBURG

Let's visit another of the most famous historic sites in America and learn what teen volunteers do to give visitors a memorable aesthetic experience. Colonial Williamsburg, in Virginia, is one of the largest museums of living history in the United States. Unless you live nearby, you won't be able to volunteer for its program. While not every historic site offers a teen volunteer program like that at Colonial Williamsburg, a visit should give you a "feel" for what can happen and what this kind of volunteering can mean for you.

We'll talk with Geales Sands, who is in charge of the volunteer work there. Here are some questions you might ask her—and her answers.

Q. How old are the Williamsburg volunteers, and what do they do?

A. We have 115 junior interpreters, all between the ages of 9 and 18, working in eight programs. Our visitors ask, "What did kids do before basketball and computers?" And our interpreters show them what children in the 18th century would have done. They do chores, help in the garden and the kitchen, play with hoops and sticks. They play checkers, huckle-buckle-beanstalk and dance.

Q. How can I get into the program?

A. We have lots more kids who want to participate than we have space for. In January and February, we host the "Volunteer Expo." All our departments that use volunteers come and acquaint the community with volunteer opportunities. The most popular area is our youth programs. We tell you about the differences among the programs. We ask you to fill out an application—and not let Mom do it. You can apply to any two of our eight programs. So you need to go to the tables and discover whether you want to be a youth recruit dancer or a kid in the Geddy House, or if you want to be in the Powell House or in historic buildings or at the Rural Trades site. You really have a smorgasbord of things to choose from.

Q. How do you decide who gets in?

A. It's just as if you were applying for a regular job. The program managers choose those who seem the most interesting and best fit our needs. You can come back year after year. And because you're seasoned and trained, you can do more each year. You can interpret a house you're working in—telling the visitors about what they are seeing in the living room or the dining room or whatever.

Q. Are all the volunteer jobs in houses?

A. No. For example, Rural Trades is an outdoor site where we have turkeys and a windmill where they grind grain into flour. We also have a basket maker and a cooper and a big garden the kids help out in. Here you have to be 13 and older because it's hard, outdoor work.

Q. What kind of training will I get?

A. In May, you go through intensive training, from 3 to 6 every day for 10 days, and a whole Saturday as well. It covers many different aspects of working as a junior interpreter. You'll have hospitality and courtesy training and you'll learn public-presentation skills. You'll also learn about the history of the colony and what was happening in Williamsburg back in the 18th century. And then you'll have training specific to the site where you'll be working.

Q. Then do I start work?

A. First you're fitted for a costume, and then you start your program. You do most of your work in the summer because that's when we have the most children visiting.

Q. How many days a week will I work? How many hours a day?

A. After your training, you work 8 to 12 hours a week, usually in 4-hour shifts. You don't work every day, for a variety of reasons. One is so we can give more teens the opportunity to do it.

Q. How many kids apply for these positions?

A. Last year, we had 85 applicants for only 20 openings, so we had to turn away 65 kids. And we restrict the program to teens from the immediate Williamsburg area.

Q. What's in it for me? What will I get out of it?

(Courtesy: The Colonial Williamsburg Foundation, Williamsburg, VA)

Two teen volunteers practice games behind the Geddy House in Colonial Williamsburg.

A. You gain historical knowledge that you wouldn't get from reading a textbook. You're actually practicing living history. And you gain lots of poise and self-confidence. I have seen an 11-year-old come to a crowd of 30 kids older than she was and have them in the palm of her hand.

When you teach visiting kids an 18th-century game, or show them how to make ribbon rosettes or use a quill pen, your job as a

(Courtesy: Colonial Williamsburg Foundation, Williamsburg, VA)

Once volunteers at Colonial Williamsburg reach 14 years of age, they can apply for paid positions as peer teachers. In this photo, a peer teacher interprets behind the Geddy House. The Geddy Foundry is in the background.

junior interpreter is to get those kids involved—not to just perform for them. That gives you great satisfaction.

Q. What will I have to give up to do this?

A. In the summer, you might have a sports conflict. And as you get older, when you're 16 or so, it's awfully tempting to get a job that pays.

Q. Do you have any jobs that pay?

A. Each site that uses the juniors has two peer teachers. They are teens who've come up through the program and then get paid to supervise the younger volunteers. You can apply for this once you're 14.

Q. What else do I give up?

A. You might have to give up some holidays—like Thanksgiving, Christmas, Easter, spring break and so on—because we try to open some of these sites when we know a lot of families will be visiting.

Q. Will volunteering here help with my college and job applications?

A. People looking for references are likely to go right to your program manager. A counselor at a local school told me that when she sees that a student was a junior interpreter, she knows that will be noticed at every college it goes to. It's a wonderful experience and kids who've been through it know their history and know how to work.

At many historic sites, you are not part of the scenery or behind the scene—you help *maintain* the scene. Across the country at historic homes, mills, one-room schoolhouses and railroad stations, among others, teen volunteers spend many summer days clearing undergrowth, pruning shrubbery, cleaning up litter, painting fences and exterior walls and doing other basic exterior maintenance. (For more information on one national program that matches teens to this kind of work, see the **"Landmark Volunteers"** section in chapter 8.)

CHAPTER FIVE

Volunteering in the Performing Arts

*W*hen we discuss volunteering in such performing arts as theater, music and dance, we must define what we mean by volunteering—or community service—carefully. For the purposes of this book, community service in these arts does not include acting, performing or dancing for a paying audience, no matter how much of it you do for no pay. Performing may be personally very rewarding, but it doesn't really fit the definition of community service. Rather, even if you have talent for onstage performance, what counts in this context is what you do as a volunteer in community service to help a nonprofit organization (which is what most regional theaters and dance companies are) present its productions to the community.

A SYMPHONY OF OPEN HOUSES, SHOW HOUSES AND ARTS DAYS

Cathy McClelland, coordinator of teen volunteers at the Baltimore Symphony, says teens contribute to her organization in many ways. They work at the "Decorator's Show House," a fund-raiser that brings in about $200,000 a year. "The Symphony Associates, the volunteer group, takes over a house for three months," she says, "and decorators come in and decorate the house any way they see fit. Then the kids as well as a lot of other volunteers staff the house, work in the boutique, work in transportation, work as a host or hostess. Whatever jobs need to be filled by volunteers, these kids do that."

The teen volunteers also work at musical open houses, when the Baltimore Symphony opens its doors to the public. One is "Arts Day," usually celebrated on the first Saturday in October. The public is invited to meet the musicians and the teens help with everything from giving directions to helping a child try a violin. "It all depends on where they need help," says McClelland.

Teens also work at the "Musical Open House" in the spring. Parents bring their children to meet musicians and listen to them play their instruments. A teen volunteer is placed as an assistant to each musician, ready to help in any way needed. In addition, the teen volunteers host "Artscape," an annual, four-day celebration of all the arts, at Symphony Hall.

Teen volunteers also work with the symphony's education department in a program called "Arts Excell." This pilot project brings together Baltimore City, Baltimore County and local private schools. The project sends some 40 musicians into 11 schools for the full school year to show how music can be integrated into the curriculum. The teen volunteers set up all the materials needed for delivery to the schools for the musicians to use in teaching each class.

TEEN BECOMES AMSOV REGULAR PANELIST

High school senior Tamika Peters speaks of volunteering with the Baltimore Symphony: "I go in Saturdays and Sundays and holidays, whenever it's something interesting. I usher for the programs and help with the Open House, when people come by to see the house and give money to the symphony." Tamika also helps bring new student volunteers into the Young Adults Program, promising them it will be "a fun experience for anyone who likes music."

At Open House rehearsals, Tamika has helped serve dinners. She became so well known as a teen volunteer that she was asked to be a panelist at a convention of the American Major Symphony Orchestra Volunteers (AMSOV). "I answered basic questions about why I volunteered, and what I get from it," she says. "Everybody liked what I said, so I became one of AMSOV's regular panelists."

You gain a lot when you are an insider. High school senior Brian Edmonds, another volunteer with the Baltimore Symphony, says that he enjoys the chance to speak to interesting people—the directors, conductors and musicians—and interact with them.

"Also," says Brian, "I enjoy helping somebody else learn something, like helping the kids pick up the instruments and learn how to play them. Many people just don't take the time to do things like that."

Can teenagers make calls asking for donations? They do in Baltimore. Teen Coordinator McClelland says the teens work with the development office in soliciting money from symphony patrons. "It's not cold calling," she notes, "because these people have all given before." They also make thank-you calls to people who have given for the first time, thanking them for contributing.

"That's the most fun for them," says McClelland, "because people don't expect to get thank-you calls." In recent years, one of the teen volunteers has regularly stood up in front of the orchestra members to remind them how important it is that they participate in annual giving. Another speaks to a meeting of the symphony staff, giving the same message.

I try to get people to give money for the symphony. It needs money to support certain events. We make phone calls to get people to pledge.

—Teen Volunteer Brian Edmonds,
Baltimore Symphony

(Courtesy: Baltimore Symphony Orchestra, Baltimore, MD)

Fund-raising is essential for the success of the Baltimore Symphony. Tamika Peters (bottom left), Derek Noel (top left), Brian Edmonds (top right), and Katie Redhead (bottom right) have all worked the phones encouraging people to pledge their support.

"WE DESPERATELY NEED INTERNS"

Similar opportunities can be found in theaters around the country. For example, let's look at the Stamford Center for the Arts in Stamford, Connecticut, which maintains the Palace Theater (offering full, live stage productions) and two art galleries. Teens who are mostly high school seniors spend volunteer time assigned to specific departments of the center: community relations, marketing, audience development, fund-raising and even accounting. If you volunteer there, what will you be doing?

"Everything the rest of us do," says Jennie Ober, whose duties there include coordinating the volunteers, "from correspondence to filing to helping create new proposals to research." Ober makes the point that you learn a business, but a business that is different from the retail industry, in which most teens have some experience by the time they are 16 or 17. The arts, she says, are unique because they depend so heavily on working together to achieve an end. Fund-raising, for example, makes a strong impact on production and on the box office.

Altogether, working as a volunteer in a theater company gives you a chance to see a project from initial conception as just an idea through to final production. "You see how many bodies it takes to actually get something done," says Ober. "All the different things are constantly working out of one another's pockets and trying to be supportive of each other. And you gain an understanding of when what you need to accomplish must take a back seat to what someone else needs to accomplish in order to meet the goal of the organization."

We always have projects that are much bigger than we can accommodate. That's part of being a nonprofit organization and being a theater. We desperately need interns and they're not easy to find. When teenagers see the executive director helping to get out a mailing, I think it speaks volumes to them.

—Jennie Ober, Stamford Center for the Arts,
Stamford, Connecticut

In almost any regional theater or dance company, the job most commonly filled by volunteering teenagers is ushering. In California, the Old Globe Theatre, located in the heart of San Diego's famed Balboa Park, maintains one of the largest corps of volunteer ushers anywhere—52 teams of 21 to 23 ushers each. Two of the teams are entirely teenage, including the team captains.

What do they do? Some maintain specific posts in the theater, to give directions and be helpful. Some pass out programs, while others handle the complimentary hearing-aid kits that are provided and still others show patrons to their seats.

What's in it for you if you volunteer in a theater like this? First, you get to see the show. Second, as the Old Globe's volunteer coordinator, Joyce Buxbaum, says, "It teaches you customer service and customer relations. You have to act in a particular manner that is very mature. It gives you the responsibility of dressing accordingly and being on time and greeting the patrons coming in." The commitment, Buxbaum says, is one that she finds "a lot of teenagers are very willing to take on."

But that's not all. Teens at the Old Globe volunteer their time during holiday and spring breaks to go into the office during business hours to help with mailings and to handle other administrative tasks.

HELPING THE DANCE IN A CULTURAL MECCA

Eugene, Oregon, is a small city of some 150,000 people, but it boasts a reputation as a "cultural mecca" with more professional arts organizations than any other city its size in America. The Eugene Ballet Company's season runs for 36 weeks a year, yet its full-time, paid staff (not counting dancers) numbers only six people. How do they do it? By using volunteers, many of whom are teenagers.

Eugene Ballet's teens not only usher, they also help the staff get out mailings, they answer phones and help with filing. They organize and run tea parties for the young dancers. They handle the details of fund-raising events, from parking cars to serving refreshments and cleaning up. And, as Sandy Naishtat, financial manager of the company, says, "none of this has anything to do with ever getting on the stage."

NEWSLETTERS AND HAND-SEWN SMOCKING

You will find a similar story in other regions. In Minneapolis, Minnesota, at the Tyrone Guthrie Theatre, one of the pioneer regional companies, ushering is the most heavily populated volunteer effort for teens. One reason is that it can be done in the evening, outside of school hours.

But if you have skills the theater needs and the scholastic qualifications to gain approval from your school authorities, you can do what one Minneapolis high school senior did. She arranged her class schedule so she could spend half days for an entire semester volunteering at the Guthrie. There she worked regularly in the office and took on such assignments as interviewing the organization's leaders and some of the performers as well as costume and set designers for articles in the theater's newsletter.

Another talented volunteer worked through the summer after 11th grade in the Guthrie's costume department, where she was acclaimed for the beautiful smocking she hand sewed on elaborate costumes.

In a major regional theater like the Guthrie, "you can always stand to learn something," says Jeff Hall-Flavin, the theater's volunteer coordinator. Hall-Flavin started there as a volunteer. He says he learned something every time he gave a tour and every time he helped with a project. "The theater-makers of tomorrow," he concludes, "really should go through a program like ours. And, of course, we couldn't do all the programs we do without volunteers."

"COUNTLESS LITTLE DETAILS EVERY SINGLE DAY"

At the Cleveland Playhouse in Ohio, you can find volunteer ushers who started as teenagers and are now in their 70s. The playhouse's education department, in which you can volunteer today, dates from 1935. In a program like this, you not only help to "house manage"—that is, greet patrons, pass out programs and usher— but you also get out mailings and handle offstage chores.

In the summer, playhouse teens help in summer-camp classes for younger children. Year-round, they help the teachers of creative drama classes for fifth- to seventh-graders, and they work in such areas as the costume shop, where they help sort and store costumes.

You can find volunteer ushers who started as teenagers and are now in their 70s.

What do you get out of working as a volunteer in a long-established theater like the Cleveland Playhouse? "You get a sense of how hands-on the theater is," says the playhouse's director of educational outreach, Nancy Sirianni. "When they come here, a lot of kids have a Hollywood idea of what theater is. They don't realize the amount of business that goes on. But here you discover it's not all fun and games. You find out that department heads make photocopies. There's a lot of work—countless little details every single day to make sure the product onstage is as wonderful as it can be."

In any regional theater like the Cleveland Playhouse, you get benefits beyond just seeing a free performance where you usher, particularly if you are a budding actor or backstage worker. You also have the opportunity to watch rehearsals and to meet the artists and develop the possibility of being mentored by them.

The story is much the same at the Long Wharf Theatre in New Haven, Connecticut. Ushering is the chief volunteer activity for teens. The theater purposely reaches out to high-school students. "Our only requirement," says Jennifer Powers, audience services manager, "is that you dress nicely and show up on time." Powers reports that there are no age or grade-level limitations. "We want somebody who is responsible enough to help out. The youngest usually are 14 or 15," she notes.

In many theaters like the Long Wharf, teens can work in areas other than ushering. Teens who start as ushers are welcome to move into internships in which they work backstage in costumes, props and sets. "This gives you," says Powers, "a sense of what theater production ought to be. It's a good introduction and you get to meet a lot of people."

Finding volunteer opportunities in dance companies is kind of catch-as-catch-can, explains John Munger of Dance U.S.A., an organization to which many dance companies belong. Of nearly 700 ballet and modern-dance companies in America, only about 60 have budgets greater than $1 million and can afford fully professional performers and staff. Others are semiprofessional, paying only their principal performers. Almost all, of any size, maintain dance schools. As part of their training, students from the schools appear onstage in supporting roles alongside the paid professionals.

The semiprofessional companies "can use all the help they can get," says Munger, "and commonly tap into their entire population with a self-invented setup." Dance-school students sell tickets and usher, and help in the office with mailings and fund-raising. For the most part, they are the teenagers who do the "volunteer" work.

This means that while you are almost certain to be welcome if you volunteer to usher or work in any nonperformance area, you are not likely to find dance companies looking for you. You must look for them (see chapter 8).

Take the giant San Francisco Ballet, for example. It boasts many, many volunteer ushers, but none is a teenager. Its coordinator of volunteers, Rudy Picarelli, says that a handful of teens who are 18 or 19 (high school seniors or very recent graduates) help with the jobs that other adult volunteers also do—the administrative work in the office, such as getting out mailings, answering phones and filing. None works backstage.

Or look at the Fort Worth–Dallas Ballet in Texas. If you call and offer to usher, it will welcome you, but it has no teen program and does not recruit teens. "You do get to see the show," says House Manager Susan Williams, "and you get a perspective on who comes to see ballet. You realize there's an administrative side, and that it's not just costumes and makeup."

Ballet Chicago is a prominent company that offers an established program for teen volunteers who are not enrolled in its school or training program as dancers. Like many others already described in the performing-arts world, these teens serve as ushers and handle countless administrative tasks, from stuffing envelopes for membership and fund-raising mailings to answering phones, filing and helping with an endless round of teas and receptions.

CHAPTER SIX

Volunteering in Visual Arts and Art Museums

*I*n some museums, you may find the training rather specialized. For example, take the Seattle Art Museum, which is actually two museums—the Downtown Art Museum and the Asian Art Museum. Teen volunteers are trained only at the Asian Art Museum. "Over a period of about six months," says Fred Wong, coordinator of the museum's teen volunteers, "they learn Asian art history. It's a very big subject, so it's hard to do the whole history from prehistoric times." Wong says this does not give the teens as much art history as an adult docent would get, but they get more of a sense of aesthetics and they get a lot of hands-on activities that relate to Asian art.

The Saturday program is the training. We practiced for half a year before we started giving tours. We began training in October, and our first tour was in April.
                    —Teen Volunteer Miya Bernson,
                              Seattle Art Museum

"My tour partner and I get together a small group of people, usually about 15," says Katie Plimpton, a high school sophomore who is a teen volunteer in the Seattle Art Museum. "We take them around the museum and we explain the art to them, using a basic theme." A

(Courtesy: Seattle Art Museum, Seattle, WA)

Miya Bernson (left), Clare Hungate-Hawk (center) and Katie Plimpton (right) take a break from telling the story of Buddha at the Seattle Art Museum.

typical theme she often chooses is symbolism—the symbols in the art. Religion is another theme. One of her tours usually takes about half an hour. She finds the length depends on how many questions people ask.

One of Katie's touring partners is eighth-grader Miya Bernson, who volunteers at the museum every other Saturday. She and Katie work together giving tours designed for organized groups that call the museum and ask for a tour. "People have been known to wander in and listen to us," she says, "when we are just practicing touring and rehearsing what we are going to say."

The biggest criterion I use is interest and passion about art. They may not do at all well in public speaking, but that's part of the training. I've turned down people who are very good at speaking but clearly are not very interested in the art.
**—Coordinator of Teen Volunteers Fred Wong,
Seattle Art Museum**

TEEN TEACHES TEACHERS

A high-school sophomore who volunteers at the Seattle Art Museum is pleased with her experience.

"I was able to lead a tour of 35 Seattle public-school teachers," says Rhianna Goans. "We interacted. They asked me questions, and I asked them what they thought this or that was used for." Rhianna took the teachers through an Oriental tomb and explained huge tigers that were on each side to scare people away. In another room, she showed them how the ancient Chinese wore mirrors to ward off evil spirits. In a third area, she explained why all the figures were elaborate with many pieces of jewelry and intricate details, while the Buddha was quite plain and had what appeared to be a bun on top of his head. "Actually," she explained, "it's a second brain, to show his overpowering knowledge."

THE MUSEUM OF FINE ARTS, HOUSTON

This museum offers a special program for juniors and seniors who attend an inner-city high school. Run by Christine Choi, who is manager of school programs in the museum's education department, the museum brings in students from Jessie Jones High School and trains them to give afternoon tours to community organizations. "That's their primary function," says Choi. "They also get to volunteer at other educational programs, like teacher workshops, family programs and special holiday events that we sponsor."

Even if they have after-school jobs or sports activities, the teens are encouraged to participate in the program. The workload ebbs and flows, Choi says, and "eventually it kind of evens out." If you volunteer in an art museum like this, you know that you are welcome even if your time is limited by soccer season or an after-school job.

A MURAL A BLOCK LONG

Sometimes your volunteering in an art museum can take you into the great outdoors and expose you to an endless stream of art patrons. That's what happened to 16-year-old Chris Anderson in the summer of 1997, when he volunteered at the Stamford Center for the Arts in Connecticut.

A wall 6 feet high and a city block long had been erected as a barrier in front of the center's Palace Theatre while it was

(Continued on page 70)

(Continued from page 69)

being remodeled. Jennie Ober, the center's coordinator of volunteers, saw the blank, gray stretch of wall as a visual-arts opportunity. The nearby Whitney Museum and Cowles Business Media office each provided grants for art supplies. Adult artist June Ahrens directed the project. And Chris found himself in charge of a bunch of kids aged 14 down to 8 who arrived from the Urban League's summer camp every morning at 9. The group worked until lunchtime or later each day for two weeks to create a vast, high-spirited mural to brighten the heart of downtown Stamford.

Chris's job was to mix paint and supervise as the kids drew each other's outlines in action poses on sheets of brown paper, then cut them out and transferred them to the wall. "I didn't even know there was an Urban League," said Chris afterward. "It was a pleasant surprise. It was nice to watch them get excited."

The young teens who painted caught the spirit of volunteering, too. "They really had to work together and make decisions together about what colors to paint and what details to put in," says Ahrens. "And being out on the street with people passing by all the time gave them a sense of pride. It was empowering and very worthwhile for them."

(Courtesy: Seattle Art Museum, Seattle, WA)

Rhianna Goans, a volunter at the Seattle Art Museum, speaks to a group of children about the Chinese Buddhist art collection.

CHAPTER SEVEN

What's in It for You?

Volunteers often come back from college to join the permanent staff.

*L*ike other volunteer work, working to promote the arts and sciences is an interesting way to meet community service requirements. It gives you the opportunity to meet and interact with paid professionals in the field as well as volunteers of all ages and backgrounds. It also offers you many other benefits. It helps you toward your future career. Even if you decide not to go into work in promoting the arts and sciences, you acquire practical knowledge you can use throughout your life.

CAREER BENEFITS

Volunteering in this field can help lead to a career. "Not only do our volunteers come back," says Maria Bagg, coordinator of volunteers at Mystic Seaport in Connecticut, "but some have never left." She says seaport volunteers often come back from college to join the permanent staff. They are welcomed because they know the place and what its expectations are.

While you may not land a permanent job in the same place where you volunteered as a teenager, you can be sure that early experience in the field of your choice can be a real advantage.

FROM VISITOR TO VOLUNTEER STAFF

"Because we're a children's museum, we've seen visitors to the museum graduate into the teen volunteer program, and then graduate into our staff," says Peggy Beidelman, coordinator of volunteers at the Chicago Children's Museum.

"We have two folks who started out in our youth program and are now regular staff," Beidelman explains. The former teen volunteers now supervise other young staff. Some attend college part time and work at the museum part time. They are likely to grow into careers as museum educators.

One volunteer coordinator, Christine Choi of the Museum of Fine Arts in Houston, even got an e-mail from a former teen volunteer who was on a field trip in Australia while majoring in biology at the Massachusetts Institute of Technology (MIT). The MIT junior was suddenly realizing that the museum was where she wanted to be. "I remember what we did junior year and I really want to do that again," she wrote. Choi helped her explore internship possibilities at museums.

High school senior Lindsey Shaginaw, a volunteer at Pittsburgh's Carnegie Museum of Natural History, found that "it's neat to talk with so many researchers and the herpetologist and see what they like about their careers. It gives me an idea of what I should be looking for in my search for colleges."

At the Denver Museum of Natural History, Teen Volunteer Coordinator Vicki Leigh finds that many students volunteer because they

(Courtesy: Denver Museum of Natural History, Denver, CO)

A group of teen volunteers from the Denver, Colorado, Museum of Natural History on a field trip to Dinosaur Ridge.

are interested in science and in culture. "Since this program started," she says, "we have consistently had a 50 percent or more return rate each year. This summer was the first year that we had some teens who started when they were just 14 and who are now going off to college. They were with us every summer." She adds that many of them have made decisions to go into science as a result of working at the museum. They have asked staff people to write letters of recommendation for them to get into college and to help them with scholarships.

Jenny Butts, a high school senior who volunteers at the Kansas Museum of History in Topeka, says her work there enabled her to sample a future career. "I'm thinking of majoring in education," says Jenny, "because I like kids a lot and it's fun to work with them. This gives me a chance to see if it's something I would really like to do."

These kids are beginning the networking process of getting into college and getting a job. Certainly I'll write recommendations. But I won't unless I feel something is good.
—**Coordinator of Volunteers Cathy McClelland,**
Baltimore Symphony

Colleges do consider how much time an applicant has spent in community service.

COLLEGE APPLICATIONS

Will your volunteer work be valuable on a college application? You bet. "It's always valuable," Maria Bagg says. "I let them know on day one. I say, you're probably not thinking about it right now, but I guarantee you that when you go to college, you're going to put down that you volunteered at Mystic Seaport Museum." Bagg notes that she files the records of evaluations of teen volunteers by their supervisors. If a college calls about one of the seaport's "alumni," she photocopies all the comments and sends them.

"I let the kids know right up front that the comments are not always wonderful," says Bagg. "If they're not cooperative, not dependable, if they're rude, if they're irresponsible, that's on their record. I want them to know that this isn't just fun and games. It *is* fun and games, but that's not all it is."

The fact is that colleges do consider how much time an applicant has spent in community service, and what kind of service it was. Often they base financial aid or scholarships at least partly on the community service record.

Colleges look at what you put back into the community around you, so that's a big motivation.
—Teen Volunteer Ellen Thompson,
Kansas Museum of History, Topeka

DISCIPLINE AND BEHAVIOR

As in many other types of volunteering, you can expect your work in the arts and sciences to give you solid experience in the discipline of the working world. The more you develop your people skills, for example, the more you learn how to practice the art of patience. You will find (if you haven't already in other situations) that handling people who are several years younger than you demands plenty of patience—especially when they come into a public place as visitors.

Peggy Beidelman, coordinator of volunteers at the Chicago Children's Museum, points out that the skills of customer service and visitor relationships come in handy as part of life. "Knowing what kind of person to be when you're dealing with someone who is on the other side of the cash register," she says, "is actually the area of greatest improvement for most teens." As you spend time dealing with the public in any museum situation, your communications skills are sharpened and fine-tuned.

Beidelman explains that the skills you learn in volunteering really depend on the organization in which you work and the type of work you do there. "For the teens who come and help with our office work," she says, "they get quite a bit of real-life skills, real job experience." If you work in this museum or one like it, you do more than work with computers. You are trained in ways to communicate in an office situation. This may include how to communicate when you are frustrated with an assignment your boss gives you, or how to deal with coworkers in a professional way.

(Courtesy: Kansas State Historical Society, Topeka, KS)

Dan Lawrence volunteers at the Kansas Museum of History in Topeka. At the Wichita Indian exhibit, he displays replicated items in an Indian suitcase, or "parafleche," which contains a buffalo bladder and scapula hoe. Many college admission offices appreciate the value of volunteer experience in a museum setting.

"You may know how to deal with your friends, your grandparents, your teachers," says Beidelman, "but when you get to work, you can't necessarily use those same coping mechanisms. You really get some insight into not just technical skill—typing and that sort of thing—but also the skills that are more subtle. I would say that's definitely a big plus."

BE RESPONSIBLE FOR YOURSELF

The adults who give you responsibility in their organizations will encourage you to take charge. "I think the important thing," says

77

Maria Bagg of Mystic Seaport, "is that the teens learn to be responsible for themselves." As an example, Bagg says she turns away mothers who call her to say their "absolutely wonderful, talented and mature" teen wants to volunteer. She interrupts the flow of superlatives to suggest speaking with the teen instead of the mother. And if parents come along for an interview, she leaves them in the reception room while she talks with the candidate. "Right away, the teenager thinks, 'Hey, I'm going to have to do this for myself,' " she says.

What's in this for you, of course, is a feeling of self-worth and of responsibility. It puts you in a position where you can be frank with the interviewer about what you want to do. In conclusion, says Bagg, "When I ask the question, 'What do you think you'd like to do?' I don't have a father speaking up and saying, 'Well, he's always been interested in wood carving.' "

PRACTICAL EXPERIENCE

Volunteering in almost any organization can give you real, hands-on experience as opposed to reading or hearing about it from your friends or your guidance counselor. Veronique Le Mell, executive director of the Jamaica Arts Center in Queens, New York, explains, "These kids are getting work experience, which is really important. It's doing something because you want to and because it's what's expected of you."

Le Mell points out that when you volunteer, you are not in a school situation. You do not have a teacher, but you do have a supervisor. "We get kids," she explains, "who don't understand that if your workday starts at 10, that doesn't mean you come in at 11 just because there's no teacher watching you and attendance isn't being taken. It's learning about responsibility, self-reliance and the real world. The teens are dealt with like another staff member; they're *not* dealt with like a student."

Since this is their first work experience, they discover the basics of a job: getting here on time, being part of a group, performing when they might not feel like it, communicating with other people, making friends and associations.
      —**Manager of Volunteer Programs Judy Kupfer,**
            Chicago Museum of Science and Industry

A GOOD PLACE TO HANG

Karen Turner, director of special programs, discusses what teen volunteers get out of working at the Fort Worth Museum of Science and History. "This is a safe, fun place for them to spend a lot of time. Most of these teens don't want to be at home, they want to be out where they can meet peers, but they want some place safe."

Volunteering gives you a first opportunity with job skills. Once you accomplish a task or do some volunteer work for a while, you feel a real sense of achievement. It can be very good for your self-esteem.

Even if you volunteer because it is required by your school, you are more than likely to stay at the job because you truly enjoy it. "The teen volunteers will tell you," says Turner, "that they like making new friends, and they like hanging out here. This is a good place to be."

LEARNING BEYOND SCHOOL

The fact is that you can broaden your education and your general knowledge by doing volunteer work in many fields—perhaps more so in the arts and sciences than in many others. You can even discover that a subject you thought was a big bore is far from it. Mary Madden, director of education at the Kansas Museum of History in Topeka, has noticed that. "One of the most rewarding benefits of this program," she says, "is to get letters from kids who have had trouble with history in school and discovered they like history

(Courtesy: Fort Worth Museum of Science and History, Fort Worth, TX)

In Texas, volunteers at Fort Worth's Museum of Science and History learn valuable job skills such as dealing with the public over the phone.

because of their experience here."

Another benedit of volunteering in a museum is that you have access to parts of the facility that the public does not get to see. You work in a professional environment. Most entry jobs for teenagers are business places like McDonald's, where, as Madden observes, "you're not going to be working with people who have their doctorates. Here, you do get a good crash course in history."

What is in it for me is the experience of seeing how the working world works. The average person who goes into the museum doesn't realize how much goes into an operation like that. It's not done in a day by any means.

—Ninth-Grade Volunteer Tyler Kaye,
Naval Undersea Museum, Keyport, Washington

DEVELOP LEADERSHIP AND COMMUNICATIONS SKILLS

You also get the chance to develop your leadership and communications skills. Christine Choi, school-programs manager in Houston's Museum of Fine Arts, observes, "A lot of teens are shy at first. They're not used to speaking in front of large groups—kids they don't know and multiage groups."

Choi's chief concern is that teens are able to communicate with strangers in a positive manner. She is not as concerned with whether they have a background in art history. "We want our visitors to have fun and to come back to the museum," she says. "That's our priority, so our docents have to be really engaging and friendly and warm."

Teachers tell me that the teens in our program are so much more comfortable getting up and talking in front of a group. They have a lot more confidence. They're good speakers.
—Teen Volunteer Coordinator Sherri Rawstern, Dakota Prairie Museum, Aberdeen, South Dakota

Choi expects her teen volunteers to have some leadership and decision-making skills. "That gets built in as they go along," she says, "because lots of things are going to happen, and they are the leaders." The fact is that when you work as a docent, in the eyes of the visitors you are a member of the museum staff. Therefore, whatever you do or whatever you say is what the visiting kids are going to follow. "We try to prepare our teen volunteers for unexpected things," says Choi, "and we help give them the confidence to be able to make decisions."

81

As our program has grown, we have been able to offer the teen volunteers who've been with us a few years the opportunity to do some supervision.
—Coordinator, Teen Docent Program, Cathy Andreychek,
Carnegie Museum of Natural History, Pittsburgh

SENSE OF PRIDE

There's something even deeper that you can get out of volunteering: a sense of pride, almost of shareholding, in the organization for which you work. "The teen volunteers get behind the scenes," Choi explains, "into places that the public does not get access to, like a security area and the preparations area where the framing is done and where people actually touch the art." In this kind of volunteering, you feel as if you are part of the museum. And you soon find that the museum staff appreciates the fact that there are teens who are actually interested in spending free time at the museum. Knowing this gives you a sense of pride in what you do. You begin to recognize staff members and have a rapport with them.

In most places where you volunteer, you get certain advantages. As a docent or interpreter in a museum, you will probably be allowed to come in at no cost whenever you want to and you will probably even be allowed to bring in family members. As an usher in a theater or concert hall, you can see and hear the performances free of charge. Like all staff people, you will have a badge bearing your name, and you may wear a special T-shirt, smock or some other kind of "uniform" when you give tours, so people know who you are. "It's fun that you feel proprietorship over the museum and you can talk about works of art with confidence," says Choi. "You get a lot out of it in that way."

If you're wondering at the outset whether you are going to find your volunteer work interesting and worthwhile, check on how much turnover there is in the place where you volunteer. "We don't have a whole lot of movement in and out," says Wendy Coones, teen volunteer coordinator at the Fort Worth Museum of Science and History. "When the kids come into the program, they can stay until they're 17. We keep the numbers small so that they can get as much out of the place as they want." Coones reports that a number of part-time staffers at the museum started as volunteers. One who recently departed for college had started volunteering at 14, moved up to an internship and then was on the part-time staff. She had worked in history collections and had redesigned one of the exhibits. "Some of the part-timers who are former volunteers even do taxidermy in the science department," says Coones.

IS IT RIGHT FOR YOU?

The way to answer this question is to look at the advantages and satisfactions that you can get from volunteering, and the disadvantages and dissatisfactions you may have to face. When you have reviewed some of these, you can take a quiz to determine if this area is right for you.

ADVANTAGES AND SATISFACTIONS

Working with people who help give the public its aesthetic experience helps you find out whether you want to concentrate on this field when you get to college and later in your lifework. If you are considering but not sure about being a teacher, librarian, museum or art gallery curator, historian, naturalist, archaeologist or paleontologist, for example, you can find out before you make a commitment in terms of your education. Finding out can save you time and money.

Let's look at some of the other advantages and satisfactions you gain.

Handling Responsibility. In most of the situations described in this book, you get good practice in taking on responsibility. As you do so successfully, you gain a second advantage: You improve your self-image or self-esteem. You get to know your own capabilities and limitations.

Gaining Recognition. With your voluntary service, you make new friends not only among your peers but also among the adult volunteers and staff people with whom you work. Getting their recognition and approval can be especially valuable. For example, they can help you when you need recommendations or references to put on college or job applications.

Find out before
you make a
commitment.

Making New Friends. Volunteering in any of the arts areas introduces you to new people beyond your usual group—some your own age and others who are older or younger than you.

Tuition-free Classes. Some museums, galleries and arts centers that offer classes and study programs for a fee are glad to give full scholarships to volunteers in exchange for the amount of work they do.

DISADVANTAGES AND DISSATISFACTIONS

There are some negatives you should think about.

No Pay. You must weigh the advantages you will get from a volunteer job against the disadvantage of giving up time that you could be using to earn money.

Weekends. Most of the places where you are likely to volunteer are open to the public on Saturdays and Sundays, or give performances on those days. So you will probably have to expect to give up at least three or four hours on either or both days once or twice a month. This may cut into your social life, sports events or other recreation. It may even cost you some sleeping-in time.

I really loved working with the people. It's important to be able to work with and understand people who are older and younger. It's a good lesson for life to feel that kind of equality. That's something the museum has provided that I wouldn't have gotten anywhere else.

—Teen Volunteer Laurel Simmons, Fort Worth Museum of Science and History

SELF-QUIZ

Now ask yourself some questions.

- Are you interested in the work of creative people—such as musicians, dancers, actors and artists?
- Are you the creative type yourself—play one or more instruments, draw, paint, sculpt, write, compose music, act, dance?
- Does the field of education appeal to you? Are you thinking of becoming a teacher?
- Do you like to learn about history and tell others about it?
- Do you enjoy learning about natural history and its related fields, such as paleontology and anthropology?
- Can you speak to a mixed group of strangers of all ages?
- Are you an organizer? A leader?
- Are you computer literate? Do you know word processing?
- Can you commit anywhere from 30 to 200 hours of the school year, or 50 hours of your summer, to this work?
- Can you balance your schoolwork, a paying job and this volunteer job and not "spread yourself too thin"?
- Can you ask questions? When you don't grasp a task or question, are you willing to say you don't understand?
- Are you willing to try volunteering in an area you may not previously have known much about?

CHAPTER EIGHT
Where to Find Opportunities

Start your search by checking with teachers and guidance counselors at your school. Ask history teachers about local historic buildings and sites, art teachers about galleries and museums, music teachers about orchestras.

Call or stop in at the reference desk at your public library. They should know about organizations and institutions in your area.

Put your phone book to work. See the Yellow Page listings under *Museums* (that's where art galleries are listed, too), *Orchestras and Bands* and *Theaters.* Dance companies are listed under *Dancing Instruction,* perhaps because most companies include a school. If you cannot find a particular group (not all maintain phones in their names), call your local chamber of commerce. People there know where to find the nonprofit organizations.

Network with your parents, relatives, friends and parents of friends. And don't forget to search the Internet for the websites of museums, symphonies, dance companies and regional theaters. It can give you many ideas on doors to knock on.

If you cannot find just what you want, you can always try creating your own opportunity. Asked if they use teenage volunteers, a surprising number of organizations—theaters and museums especially—often reply, "We don't and we wish we did, but we don't have the time or the personnel to go out and get them. If they came to us, we'd be glad to have them." That sounds like a door you don't have to knock on. It is already open.

Even in Atlanta, Georgia, a city in which community service is a requirement for graduation from all public high schools, the Atlanta Symphony offers no regular program for teenage volunteers.

LANDMARK VOLUNTEERS

If you would like to spend two weeks of your summer in volunteer work somewhere away from home, find out about Landmark Volunteers. To qualify, you must be at least 14½ years old and entering 10th, 11th or 12th grade in September. The opportunities, in more than 40 locations across America, are in historical, cultural, environmental and social service organizations. They range from working with the Britt Gardens Music and Arts Festivals in Medford, Oregon, to the Boston Symphony at Tanglewood in Massachusetts, from Historic New Harmony (a museum community of 14 restored homes) in Indiana to Mystic Seaport in Connecticut and Colonial Williamsburg in Virginia. (The Mystic and Williamsburg opportunities are in addition to those for people who live near the sites, which have already been described in this book.)

The work is basically manual, including maintaining buildings and grounds, building fences, painting and other improvements—most of it outdoors. Some indoor assignments may be included, such as helping with research, working on collections, conducting surveys or serving as an usher.

(Continued on page 88)

If you donate your services through Landmark Volunteers, you may do maintenance work on buildings and grounds at various places throughout the United States. In this picture, Jenni (top), Stan (center) and Tara are painting a horse barn on Santa Cruz Island off the California coast.

(Courtesy: Landmark Volunteers, Sheffield, MA)

(Continued from page 87)

You (or your parents or guardians) pay a tax-deductible contribution, plus travel expenses, for the two-week period. For details, contact:

Landmark Volunteers
P.O. Box 455
Sheffield, MA 01257
Phone: (413) 229-0255
Fax: (413) 229-2050
Home page: http://www.volunteers.com
E-mail: Landmark@volunteers.com

APPLICATIONS AND INTERVIEWS

What do you say when you call? Ask for the person who coordinates volunteers. You may not get that person on the first call because all coordinators are busy. Be sure to leave a message with your name and phone number, saying you want to find out about volunteering. Ask if you need an application form and if the coordinator can mail you one. Or you may offer to stop by and pick up the form.

If no one calls back within a few days, call again. Do not get discouraged. Persistence pays off. If you have decided on a particular place where you want to volunteer, keep at it. You may find that they accept applications only at certain times or seasons of the year.

If you can't get in right away, ask to be placed on a waiting list. Be sure to write thank-you letters that follow up on your calls. While you're thinking of *them,* you want *them* to be thinking of you.

When you are interviewed, feel free to ask questions. What kind of training program will you have to go through? How many training meetings a week, for how many weeks? How many teen volunteers are in the program? Is there a period of probation, and how long is it?

Let your interviewer know that you have thought about your volunteering. Make him or her aware that you want to know what you are getting into in the same sense that he or she wants to know about you.

GET A RÉSUMÉ READY

Looking for a volunteer job is like looking for a paying job. You want to make the best possible impression. Handing a résumé to your interviewer makes two points:

1. that you have been somewhere and done something, and

2. that you know how to think about where you have been and what you have done.

What goes into your résumé? Your full name, address, age, grade in school and school activities (e.g., Key Club, drama club, sports teams, science club, 4-H Club, publications, etc.). And be sure to include part-time jobs, from baby-sitting to delivering newspapers to mowing lawns and shoveling snow. You want the reader of your résumé to see how well-rounded you are.

HOW DO YOU LOOK?

Be sure to write thank-you letters that follow up on your calls.

Somebody said, "You get only one chance to make a good first impression." Dress for it, in clean, freshly pressed clothing. Make sure your hands and fingernails are clean. Shampoo. If you have short hair, it should be trimmed and well combed. If you have long hair, wear it in a braid or ponytail. Make it clear you know you shouldn't come to work with your hair flying in the breeze.

We're not looking for straight-A students. During the interview we stress that they can be fired. We tell them that they must treat it like a job. When they apply for a paid job, we will offer a letter of recommendation for employment.
—Director of Education Mary Madden,
Kansas Museum of History, Topeka

Finally, here's some advice from two teens you have met in this book. "I think that no matter where you're working or for what reasons," says Laurel Simmons, a 15-year-old volunteer at the Fort Worth Museum of Science and History, "you should be working because it's something you're really interested in. It should be something you enjoy doing."

Ellen Thompson, a high school senior and volunteer at the Kansas Museum of History in Topeka, agrees. "Find something you feel really comfortable in," she urges. "The first place you volunteer

(Courtesy: Kansas State Historical Society, Topeka, KS)

Alicia Madison enjoys sharing her knowledge with the public at the Kansas Museum of History in Topeka. Here, Alicia discusses reproduction items from the Oregon Trail exhibit with interested patrons. Part of this display contains lye soap, a candle mold and a cup and ball game.

may not necessarily offer something that you want to do for a long time. Do something you enjoy so you're not dreading it, because then it won't be worthwhile. Start early. In most states, you can't get a paying job until you're 16. So when you've got that free time at 15, go volunteer. It'll count almost as job experience when you apply for a paying job."

GLOSSARY

Aesthetics. The study or philosophy of the beautiful and judgments about beauty.

Anthropologist. One who studies the human species in relation to various physical, environmental, social and cultural aspects.

Artifact. Any item made by a human as a product of civilization or, more specifically, of artistic endeavor; loosely, any item used for educational purposes in a museum or exhibition.

Capstan. A vertical drum that can be turned to wind cable or rope and raise or lower a weight.

Cooper. One who makes or repairs wooden barrels, casks or tubs.

Culture. The customary beliefs and traits, as well as social forms, of a group.

Docent. A museum guide and teacher.

Eclectic. Made up of elements from a variety of sources.

Herpetologist. An expert in the branch of zoology that deals with amphibians and reptiles.

Home-schooled. Taught at home rather than in a formal academic setting.

Humanities. The human elements that make up any people's culture: their language, music, religion, philosophy, literature, arts and history, as opposed to the scientific and technological aspects of life.

Intangible Something that cannot be touched; (adjective) non-physical.

Myriad. Having many aspects or elements.

Paleontologist. One who studies past geological periods as known from fossil remains.

Philosophy. Broadly, the pursuit of wisdom; the search for understanding of values and reality.

Symbiosis. The living or working together of two dissimilar organisms in a relationship that is mutually beneficial.

SUGGESTIONS FOR FURTHER READING

The *World Book Encyclopedia* provides interesting articles on art and the arts, museums and orchestras.

For insight into the state of the humanities today, be sure to read *What's Happened to the Humanities?* edited by Alvin Kernan and published by the Princeton University Press in 1997.

The following books will help give you a broad understanding of volunteerism and opportunities in community service.

Berkowitz, Bill. *Local Heroes: The Rebirth of Heroism in America.* Lexington, MA: Lexington Books (D.C. Heath), 1987.

Buckley, William F., Jr. *Gratitude: Reflections on What We Owe to Our Country.* New York: Random House, 1990.

Coles, Robert. *The Call of Service: A Witness to Idealism.* Boston: Houghton Mifflin, 1993.

Daloz, Laurent A., Cheryl H. Keen, James P. Keen, and Sharon Daloz Parks. *Common Fire: Lives of Commitment in a Complex World.* Boston: Beacon Press, 1996.

Ellis, Susan J., and Katherine H. Noyes. *By the People: A History of Americans as Volunteers.* San Francisco: Jossey-Bass, 1990.

_____. *The Volunteer Recruitment Book.* Philadelphia: Energize, Inc., 1994.

Grashow, Mark. *How to Make New York a Better Place to Live.* New York: City and Company, 1994.

Griggs, John, ed. *Simple Acts of Kindness: Volunteering in the Age of AIDS.* New York: United Hospital Fund of New York, 1989.

Lewis, Barbara. *The Kid's Guide to Service Projects.* Minneapolis: Free Spirit, 1993.

Luks, Allan, with Peggy Payne. *The Healing Power of Doing Good: The Health and Spiritual Benefits of Helping Others.* New York: Fawcett Columbine, 1991.

Olasky, Marvin. *Renewing American Compassion.* New York: The Free Press (Simon & Schuster), 1996.

Salzman, Marian, and Teresa Reisgies. *150 Ways Teens Can Make a Difference.* Princeton, NJ: Peterson's Guides, 1991.

Spaide, Deborah. *Teaching Your Kids to Care: How to Discover and Develop the Spirit of Charity in Your Children.* Secaucus, NJ: Carol Publishing Group, 1995.

Tarshis, Lauren. *Taking Off: Extraordinary Ways to Spend Your First Year Out of College.* New York: Fireside (Simon & Schuster), 1989.

Wuthnow, Robert. *Acts of Compassion: Caring for Others and Helping Ourselves.* Princeton, NJ: Princeton University Press, 1991.